MASTERING OPTIONS TRADING

Mastering Options Trading

WILLIAM VINCENT

Contents

Chapter 1: Introduction to Options Trading

Options trading provides substantial leverage, which can significantly multiply the returns on a trade. In essence, a call buyer is betting that the stock price will rise, thus making the option more valuable. Conversely, a put buyer bets on a price drop, protecting against downside risk. Both call and put buyers possess the right to exercise the option. When exercised, this allows the purchaser to buy the underlying stock at the strike price, giving the option its intrinsic value. Trading a call is a bullish trade, whereas selling a call after purchasing can be interpreted as a bearish move.

Options form a cornerstone of Wall Street and the broader financial market. Acquiring the skill to trade options is a valuable tool for achieving financial independence. Prior to delving into options trading, several key concepts must be understood to prevent potential burnout: the Greeks, which are the value indicators of an option; the impact of volatility on trades; and the various options trading strategies based on the stock's movement. The greatest barrier to entry in options trading is often the complex terminology. However, mastering these concepts is essential to harnessing options for financial gain.

1.1 What are Options?

Options are financial contracts that grant the right, but not the obligation, to buy or sell an asset at a predetermined price. These tradable contracts are predominantly used for speculation or hedging by professional money managers and traders. Broadly, an option is a type of derivative, as its payoff profile is linked to the price dynamics of the underlying asset. Derivatives mirror the price behavior of a different type of asset, known as the underlying asset. Consequently, derivatives derive their value from the price fluctuations of this underlying asset.

Key characteristics of options contracts include the expiration date, which is the deadline by which the option must be exercised, and the strike price, which is the predetermined price. Options can be categorized as follows:

- **Call Option**: Grants the holder the right to purchase the underlying asset at the strike price on a specified date.
- **Put Option**: Permits the holder to sell the underlying asset at the strike price on or before a set date.

These rights can be exercised for a fee known as the option price or premium. Several factors influence the option price, including the holding period, the underlying asset's price, the strike price, interest rates, the time until expiration, and the market's implied volatility. Options are also classified into two general categories:

- **Vanilla Options**: Standard options with straightforward terms that are traded on an exchange.
- **Exotic Options**: Options with more complex terms and conditions, which are less commonly traded.

Benefits and Risks of Options Trading

When considering options trading, understanding the benefits and risks is crucial for making informed decisions. Here are some commonly cited benefits of options trading:

1. **Leverage**: Options trading allows traders to control a significant amount of equity with a relatively small amount of money.
2. **Hedging and Portfolio Protection**: Options strategies can effectively protect a portfolio against market downturns.
3. **Trading Income**: Selling options can generate steady income, supplementing other income streams.

However, options trading also entails certain risks:

1. **High Potential Losses**: While options trading offers leverage, it also carries the risk of significant losses if trades go awry. It's essential to have a well-defined plan and strict loss limits.

2. **Complexity**: The intricate nature of options and the necessity for precise timing can be daunting for beginners.

Options trading can be a powerful tool for achieving financial goals, provided that traders understand both the benefits and risks involved. By mastering the fundamental concepts and strategies, traders can harness the potential of options trading to work towards financial freedom.

Chapter 2: Fundamental Strategies for Options Trad

Understanding foundational concepts is crucial for anyone aspiring to become a professional trader. These basics are key to comprehending how options truly work. All fundamental options trading involves basic calls and puts. Mastering these two strategies is essential before advancing to more complex ones, as lacking this knowledge can be detrimental. Once these concepts are understood, more advanced modules can be beneficial if the need arises.

A call option provides the buyer with the right to purchase a stock at a specific price, known as the "strike" price, which is generally higher than the stock's current price. Exercising the option refers to buying the stock. Conversely, a put option grants the buyer the right to sell a stock at a stated price, also called the strike price. The concept hinges on knowing when to sell and when to buy. There are multiple methods to determine this, given that assignments can vary. For example, if one buys a put option with a premium of $5 per share for 100 shares, the total cost of the contract is $500. If the stock price falls below $100, the buyer avoids losses, as they can still sell the stock at the strike price, even if the market price is $80.

Call and Put Options

Options trading, often referred to as the options market, is a special hedging tool that significantly enhances investors' leverage. If investors use options in line with exchange rate fluctuations, they can achieve unlimited profits with limited capital. Options include call options and put options, commonly utilized in foreign exchange trading techniques.

A call option is a financial contract between two parties, giving the buyer the right to purchase an underlying asset at a predetermined price within a specified timeframe. The seller of the call option is obliged to sell the asset to the buyer if they choose to exercise the option. The buyer, holding the long position, can force the seller to sell the underlying asset under the agreed conditions. Conversely, a put option is a right to sell a security at a fixed or negotiated price within a specified period. The buyer of a put option acquires the right to sell but is not obligated to do so. Options can be based on various underlying assets, including stocks, bonds, and exchange-traded funds.

Covered Calls and Protective Puts

Covered calls and protective puts are two fundamental options strategies that new investors typically learn first. Despite their simplicity and standard structure, these strategies are crucial. Both allow investors to profit from significant stock and options price movements (or lack thereof) while managing their exposure to potential losses.

Incorporating Covered Calls A covered call strategy is typically employed by stock owners and can provide a cash payout if the underlying stock remains flat or appreciates slightly. However, poor stock performance can be exacerbated with the addition of a strike price. This strategy involves holding a long stock position and selling an out-of-the-money (OTM) call, reflecting the investor's expectations. Since stock prices generally rise over time, many investors use covered calls. However, dividend requirements can deter investors from using covered calls, particularly if there is a risk of the stock price remaining below the strike price until the dividend payout.

Understanding Protective Puts A protective put involves holding a long position in a stock while purchasing a put option to guard against potential losses. This strategy is akin to buying insurance for the stock. If the stock price falls, the put option increases in value, offsetting the losses from the stock. This strategy helps mitigate downside risk while retaining the potential for gains if the stock price rises.

Chapter 3: Advanced Strategies for Options Trading

In the previous sections, we explored some fundamental concepts and industry habits essential for achieving financial freedom through options trading. Although significant returns are expected, accurate use of options necessitates a thorough understanding of its operations and functions, which develops gradually. While the strategies we covered are accessible and frequently used, more advanced strategies also exist. Grasping these concepts is equally important for a comprehensive understanding of options trading.

While the basic strategies detailed earlier are excellent for becoming a successful options seller, advanced concepts can further refine a seller's approach. These strategies enable the creation of a more tailored portfolio while still offering substantial returns. Advanced trading habits and strategies are essential for adapting to the evolving financial landscape.

The ultimate goal of this course is to instill habits that facilitate repeated financial success. This chapter, along with the subsequent sections, delves into advanced strategies and the routines accompanying them. Given the rapid growth of this field, staying updated with the latest literature on systematic trading is crucial.

Straddles and Strangles

Straddles and strangles, along with time considerations, are some of the most complex factors traders face when dealing with options. Understanding these strategies and when to deploy them can significantly enhance a trader's proficiency in the options market.

Straddle Strategy A straddle involves purchasing both a call option and a put option. Traders use this strategy when they anticipate significant price changes but are uncertain about the direction. Although this strategy can be forgiving due to the cost of the two options, it is crucial to monitor time decay and the stock's implied volatility.

Strangle Strategy A strangle is similar to a straddle, but involves purchasing an out-of-the-money call option and put option. This strategy is less expensive than a straddle but requires a more substantial move in the underlying asset to be profitable. Time decay and implied volatility are important factors to consider when using this strategy.

Time Decay Time decay is a critical factor for options traders. Beginners often speculate with covered calls by selling call options on stocks they own, aiming to receive the highest premiums for options expiring in 2-4 weeks. However, minor price corrections can cause panic, leading to losses. Successful options trading often hinges on allowing time to work in the trader's favor. Much of the money in options trading comes from the time decay reducing the option price, allowing traders to keep the premium.

Iron Condors and Butterflies

Iron condors and butterflies are more advanced options trading strategies. These strategies require a sophisticated approach but can be valuable additions to a financial freedom strategy.

Iron Condor Strategy An iron condor involves trading call spreads and put spreads in the same monthly cycle on the S&P index. Typically, these trades are set up three to four months out, with calls and puts positioned 15%-20% out of the money. Iron condors can generate significant premium income. However, in volatile market environments, such as during 2008 and 2020, iron condors may be risky due to their position location and shorter time until expiration. Each iron condor position requires a $20,000 margin, making it a relatively volatile strategy.

Butterfly Strategy A butterfly is an options trade that includes calls and puts but is more suited to low-volatility environments. Unlike iron condors, butterflies involve options trading less deeply in and out of the money. This strategy offers less interest but also reduces market risk. Each butterfly position requires a margin of around $9,000, making it more accessible than iron condors, though it is used less frequently than traditional trades.

Chapter 4: Technical Analysis for Options Trading

Technical analysis is the most vital aspect of understanding options trading. It is highly demanded, and traders need to be proficient in it for effective stock trading. In options transactions, technical analysis is equally critical. One must have a thorough understanding of the tools and techniques used in technical analysis.

Technical analysis involves the analysis of share prices using statistical activities based on historical events. It is generally easier to understand and interpret compared to fundamental analysis. Despite being used in the past, it remains relevant today. The core assumption of technical analysis is that the stock market reflects all available knowledge, meaning no secondary information is available for examination as it is already factored into the stock price. This principle is grounded in intuitive behavior and is widely used to forecast stock market prices globally. Numerous types of technical studies can be performed, including probability, time series, and regression analyses.

While technical analysis focuses on price patterns and market trends, fundamental analysis involves evaluating financial entities based on earnings, revenue, reserves, and dividends. It helps in estimating a stock's intrinsic value and making informed investment decisions. Both analytical approaches are essential in the world of trading.

Support and Resistance Levels

To succeed in options trading, understanding support and resistance levels is crucial. These concepts can be depicted in the market through an options chain. Grasping them allows traders to determine the market's sentiment, including institutional beliefs. With this knowledge, traders can make better trading decisions based on current market trends.

Over time, this understanding fosters an intuitive sense of market behavior, a skill developed through studying historical support and resistance levels. This intuition eventually becomes a positive trading habit. While numerous variables influence where support and resistance levels are established, the fundamental idea is simple: historically, specific price areas have seen significant buying and selling activity. These levels could stem from fundamental reasons or technical systems used by various market participants.

The human factor plays a crucial role in creating and perpetuating support and resistance levels. Traders can make educated decisions and develop financially positive habits by identifying where heavy buying and selling have occurred historically in their chosen options.

Moving Averages

Moving averages calculate the average value of a stock's closing price over a specified period. They help smooth out stock prices, providing traders with a clear trend. Understanding moving averages is vital as they play a significant role in options trading, indicating important factors that can aid in developing better trading habits and strategies.

In options trading, contracts are typically not held for more than a year, depending on the trader's style and initial planning. When option volumes are low, moving averages may not be as significant but should not be ignored entirely. Short-term traders often use moving averages of 10, 20, or 30 days, while medium-term traders might use averages around 50-100 days. Long-term traders can use a 200-day average, and sometimes even a 365-day average for calculating long-term trends. These values are flexible and can vary from trader to trader.

In options trading, the crossing of a stock's price with its short-term moving average can indicate bullish trading, suggesting an increase in the probability of success. Conversely, when the short-term average crosses below the long-term average, it indicates a bearish trend, suggesting it might be time to sell. Applying moving averages simplifies trading decisions by indicating whether it is time to buy or sell and whether prevailing traders are safe or at risk. Moving averages help dictate trading strategies and establish rules for entry and exit points, contributing to the creation of a solid trading strategy and habit.

Chapter 5: Risk Management and Position Sizing

Options trading often focuses on mastering tried-and-true strategies, and for good reason. These strategies present actionable opportunities to capitalize on future price movements. However, no trading strategy is without risk. Fortunately, there are several strategies that can be employed to manage risk within the context of options trading. Choosing the most relevant strategy typically depends on the level of experience and specific goals of a given trader.

Furthermore, the mindset of a trader tends to revolve around potential profits. It is easy to overlook risk management in favor of potentially massive returns. The ability to manage and control risk is necessary to reach the ultimate goal of consistent profit. As mentioned earlier, it is also easy to overlook the topic of position size. Trading too large a size for one's account can cause a loss-making trade to force a liquidation of the account, ending a would-be trading career.

Position size is therefore of critical importance, regardless of the methods, styles, and markets of a trader.

In many ways, the ideas of position size, risk management, and trading habits are intertwined because it makes sense to place a smaller amount at risk during times of uncertainty or when personal lives are particularly busy. The conversation about risk management would be incomplete without a useful look at risk controls in real trades. Even the best traders experience significant drawdowns from time to time—they are a necessary part of the trading process. Many chronically unprofitable traders would have turned towards profitability if they had used better position-sizing techniques. With these three areas in mind, we can shape our position sizes to elevate profits and limit the losses for which we dearly labor. The goal of this chapter is to help with the transition from learning to trading to living the trader's lifestyle.

Importance of Risk Management

Risk management can be the key factor that determines how far one goes in the trading profession. In options trading, because strategies can vary significantly in risk, it is important to develop good risk management habits early on. One way to do this is by using diversified trading methods. Creating a solid risk management strategy will help solidify your investment habits.

At its core, trading option contracts is about managing and mitigating risk. When initiating a new option trade, consider the use of stop orders, limit orders, and market orders. Determine the maximum dollar amount you are willing to risk on any given trade size relative to your total account size. It is essential to base your investing habits on pure mathematical probabilities. If you don't have a method for setting a specific risk per trade figure, implementing the plan in a real-life scenario can be challenging. Emotions are our biggest enemy when trading or investing. This critical piece of your trading habits will define your strategies and the results you achieve. Risk per trade is simple and allows for diversification, assuming you are investing in new strategies with diversified deltas and relatively low-risk characteristics.

Position Sizing Strategies

In any type of trading, being able to size a position correctly is pivotal. A trader's selection of position size is closely linked to both the risk of ruin (the probability of losing a significant percentage of trading capital) and the risk of having a losing streak (the number of consecutive losing trades). It directly impacts the eventual trading outcome. Some position sizing strategies carry an extreme risk of ruin and offer high returns, while others reduce this risk but also significantly lower trading expectancy. A conservative position size strategy that can 'stay safe' in a hundred- or thousand-trials Monte Carlo test at a given level of expectancy is ideal. Anything else is risky business. Reducing the number of losing trades or the risk of ruin necessitates a significant reduction in position size. Therefore, slow trading complements the low number of lots traded, effectively starting from a more secure baseline.

Most traders are attracted to options due to the potential for high returns per lot. However, there is no point in trying to improve a trading system's potential to make $40,000 a year with six lots by using 12 lots and risking a lot of ruin. The current portfolio size must match that potential return. This encapsulates the difference between position size procedures and entire-portfolio sizing procedures. Position size strategies are satisfaction-based, focusing on returning a certain amount of money in a single trade, regardless of portfolio size. Entire-portfolio sizing strategies are centered on the entire portfolio. Treating assets with maturity means that the overall account value determines the level of trade, not the trading outcome. Building an account to a level where one lot of one system is 10% of the account requires resetting the system's initial point of view.

Chapter 6: Developing a Trading Plan

A trading plan is the foundation for anyone trying to achieve financial freedom through options trading. Think of your trading plan as your business plan, with you as the CEO. Would you feel confident investing in or banking with a company without goals, routines, or plans in place? Let's get started on the right foot by developing a solid trading plan.

Set Clear Goals Consider what you want to achieve and why. Are you seeking a secondary income, a primary income, or are you trading to leave a legacy for your children and grandchildren? Documenting your goals might seem unnecessary when you think you know what you want, but doing so helps reprogram the mind to focus. Goal-setting ignites a different part of the brain, similar to forming a new habit. It rewires your brain and ingrains those triggers into everyday life, encouraging you to execute your strategic trading plan.

Set a Deadline Next, consider the deadline by which you want to achieve your financial goals. Do you see it happening in 1 year, 5 years, or within a month? Time-blocking involves setting an ideal date, although this date is not set in stone. By setting a date, you actively strategize the best plan of action to achieve your goal. If it doesn't happen by that date, you have enough time to readjust and regroup.

Setting Clear Goals

Mission: Goals Setting clear goals is a crucial part of having a trading plan. Your goals should be realistic, reflecting what you aim to achieve with your trading. Instead of saying, "I will make $10,000 per month with $3,000," focus on the profit you want to achieve. Start with the "final" plan and work towards the trade. Daily entries should align with the overall plan to achieve significant profits. This approach is similar to setting goals for making a million dollars, buying a house, or any other major objective. Set the goal, then distance yourself from it and focus on building habits that make the goal easier to reach.

Creating a Routine

Getting into a routine is essential for options traders. Routine implies a regular procedure that you follow consistently. It helps form daily, weekly, and even monthly trading habits that keep you disciplined and focused on the necessary factors for success. A structured, effective routine allows you to concentrate on trading without being influenced by personal thoughts and distractions.

One of the most challenging aspects of trading is establishing and maintaining a routine. Ensure you have a routine that allows you to get to bed at the same time each night, get enough rest, and reflect on what went well and what could be improved each day. Being well-rested and relaxed enhances your ability to think clearly during the day and make better trading decisions. Just like in tournament horse racing, where long-term success requires a healthy lifestyle, the same applies to selling equity options. Ignoring these historical indications can lead to failure in both tournaments and options trading.

Chapter 7: Psychology and Discipline in Options Tr

The psychological aspect, particularly emotions such as fear and greed, significantly influences the eventual success of an investor. This is especially true for options trading, where the leverage factor compounds the problem. The risk and emotions grow exponentially along with leverage. While options are designed for hedging against sharp price fluctuations, traders often take large leveraged positions to capitalize on price movements of the underlying security, aiming to make quick money. However, they often end up losing it rapidly, sometimes their entire capital. When faced with such drawdowns and losses, traders tend to shift from greed to fear quickly and might give up trading altogether.

Therefore, traders need to be aware of the options market and overcome both fear and greed to succeed. Discipline bridges the gap between goals and accomplishments. In options trading, discipline means sticking to your plan and trading strategy, regardless of the circumstances. Whether you are participating in an Options Strategy Course, Options Training Institute, or engaging in different commodity options trading forums, the key to consistently winning money is to follow a strategic trading plan with disciplined trading habits. When you incur a loss, react appreciatively, thanking the market for the lesson. Embrace losses as opportunities to become a better trader, making it easier to rake in profits in the future.

Overcoming Emotions

Controlling emotions is crucial in trading. A trader's worst enemy is often their own emotions—fear, greed, over-optimism, and a lack of patience are potent influences of a losing streak. These emotions can drive you to enter trades you shouldn't, hold onto losing trades for too long, and sell winning trades too early. It is normal to experience a range of emotions when risking hard-earned money, but how you react to these emotions determines your success.

To control emotions, first recognize them. Phrases like "I don't know why the market went up" or "I don't know why I bought it" detach you from the reality of over-trading. Create positive trading habits through education, practice, experience, and sticking to your trading plan on every trade.

Avoid stop-loss orders at the same time overnight or during slow periods. Plan to exit early if the stock moves significantly against you. For quiet 30-day periods, consider shorter periods like two to four days. Stop over-trading, as it often stems from habit. Whether you're new to trading or can't help yourself, taking breaks and practicing is crucial. ActiveClassName describes a stock in the news and actively traded at a significant price change when the market opens. Our premise is that a stock will settle within one to four days. Day trading involves buying an at-the-money Call on the same day the underlying stock is purchased. Consult your broker about new day trading rules.

Sticking to Your Plan

Finding and implementing a plan that aligns profits with the market's direction is a critical habit for new traders. Once a plan is decided, it is essential not to deviate until a pre-determined review point. Using reliable sources like Gorilla Trades for direction can help potential traders get started. If Prime Trade Select continues to move, check trend-setting signals to see if the confirmed strength numbers justify placing trades. Regardless of market conditions, sticking to your plan is crucial.

Adopting a schedule is another important aspect of trading. A schedule dictates trading times and helps maintain consistency. Discipline to adhere to the schedule is a vital habit. Additionally, trading only the proper amount of equity in your account is crucial. A successful schedule and plan require habits that allow you to stick to these strategies. Throughout any trading day, circumstances may affect trades. Whether trades follow a pre-established plan or are influenced by external factors depends on the trader. Developing good habits today is essential for long-term success.

Chapter 8: Case Studies and Real-Life Examples

Many books dive into specific stock metrics and investment strategies, but there is immense educational value in learning from the successful and failed strategies of others. For this reason, case studies are an essential part of any Options Curriculum. These case studies examine actual options trades that were successful enough to live off of, providing details of the trade and day-to-day paper-trading updates to see how the trade could be most efficiently closed out. They also include mistakes made, lessons learned, and how processes were improved as a result. Mistakes are invaluable educational opportunities—they are what make us improve. It's better to make mistakes with fake money than real money and learn the lessons!

Here are some key case studies of trades:

1. **Trade in NFLX (April 16, 2010)**: Invested $4,085 to make $600 per trade.

2. **First Covered Call Trade in the East Class (September 2012)**: Invested $14,000 to return four-fold.
3. **Trade in DCTH**: Started as a hedge for other positions and turned a $338 investment into $2,963 in four weeks, or 767% return!
4. **Options Calendar Trade on SDS**: Closed for a 50% return in 5 business days, netting $3,832.74 in profits.
5. **Explosive Success Trade on MOV**: Demonstrated significant profitability.
6. **Trade in TBT**: Transitioned from a losing stock position to a "house bet," netting $9,474 in profits.

Successful Options Trades

Analyzing real-life trade examples is a great way to develop good trading habits. This part of the trader's mindset has a huge impact on how you perceive, act, and develop as an investor. Learning from our own trades and encouraging others to do the same is crucial.

TRADE EXAMPLE 1: APPLE INC. Our most recent trade involved recommending calls on Apple, which has now successfully closed. The in-depth analysis of why the trade was opened, the conditions that needed to be met, and the profit-taking and defensive trade tactics can be found in the original post.

TRADE EXAMPLE 2: VISA INC. Inside Bulls' Trade of the Week: Visa Inc. This example looks at a newly added official trade of the week. Similar to the first article, the comprehensive and well-argued options trading strategy can be found in the original post.

Conclusion: These case studies are the bread and butter of our weekly updates. Our mission when writing these is to give you a look into our thought process when placing a trade. After years and countless trades, we've developed a specific process that works for us, and through our detailed recaps of profitable trades, we believe it can work for you too. Most others won't be honest about every trade they place, as they always want to appear brilliant or hide a few select bad ones.

Learning from Mistakes

Mistakes in option trading can make your equity curve graph look like a very close shave all around. At this point, many strategy developers might shut down Excel in disgust and return to stock-picking. However, taking the wrong road can be useful for learning and eventually making you smile again.

We have been trading our main Covestor strategy live for six months, long enough to experience a few trading bombs. Using options means living with the possibility of quickly losing all or part of your capital if something goes wrong. Legging is a useful way of learning the point at which a trade doesn't perform. Nothing teaches better than losing money or missing out on potential gains. Real trades often evolve differently than those in back-testing, especially with options, which can be annoying. The cost of buying options is an input into the trading decision, and computers cannot fully understand those trading decisions. This approach, while seemingly error-prone, is useful and helps us improve.

Chapter 9: Conclusion and Final Thoughts

Congratulations! You have completed this Options Trading Guide. This guide was designed to give you insight into the strategies and habits you need to take control of your trading and live life on your terms. Forming these concepts into habits will empower you to become a confident and powerful trader. Over time, these habits will become the building blocks of a disciplined, resilient, and skilled trading career.

If you have followed this guide and taken action, you are well on your way to achieving steady and consistent income through options trading. However, this is just the beginning of your journey. The secrets to successful options trading go beyond the financial habits outlined in this guide. These habits are indicators of your potential for success and require a reconditioning of the mindset that many people have grown up with—one focused on consumption and leveraging debt. These habits set the stage for not only controlling your trading but also achieving financial freedom.

Recap of Key Points

By incorporating options into value investing, you can mitigate common problems faced by value investors, such as the risk of buying a falling stock due to changes in circumstances or analytical errors. This strategy also allows you to create monthly cash flows from stocks using covered calls, thereby boosting annual returns. In cases where potential profits align with your desired income, options strategies can partially substitute for stocks, especially during periods of market overvaluation.

A common obstacle that many investors overlook is over-diversifying a stock portfolio, which can reduce valuable returns and critical cash flow. Options trading, one of the most profitable strategies in the stock market, is becoming more accessible to individual investors.

Developing and maintaining the habit of selling put options involves trading based on imagination, which is key to financial success. Just as a writer approaches a writing project, an investor can envision the possible outcomes of a trade before spending any money. Understanding the potential results and risks of a trade makes it easier to develop the habit of selling options and trading with imagination.

The imagined outcomes will not operate in only one direction but will offer many possible scenarios, including the worst-case scenario. Preparing for the worst-case scenario, which is the only outcome you can truly control, is the secret to mastering options trading for a future of financial freedom.

Next Steps for Your Trading Journey

Having completed this guide, you are well on your way to transitioning to a new financial lifestyle. Traders like us focus on building wealth through a lifestyle that supports the pursuit of others' dreams while also funding our own. We hope this course has shown you the dedication and strategies needed to develop better habits for trading options.

As we conclude our journey together, here are some next steps for your trading journey:

1. **Build a Plan**: Develop a trade plan, set trade goals, negotiate them, and adjust as needed at regular intervals. Start with a short-term plan to get started and build a framework, especially if you are new to trading.
2. **Execute Trades**: Execute at least 5 trades in an actual market with your hard-earned money. Start with a ticker you have learned about or avoid making "theoretical" trades—now is the time to put your knowledge into action.
3. **Consult a Financial Advisor**: We encourage you to connect with a financial advisor to support building your own model portfolio. A model portfolio helps track different performance strategies regularly. A financial advisor will help hold you accountable to your goals.

Remember, this trading journey is a marathon, not a sprint. Use the knowledge and habits gained from this guide to build a financial lifestyle that supports the life you want to lead. Congratulations on completing this guide, and best of luck on your trading journey!